"Quick, effective marketing & motivational training sessions driving you to success"

It Will Always Be This Time

Vol. 25 In The *Sub 4 Minute Extra Mile* Series

by

Dr. Ted Ciuba

It Will Always Be This Time

Vol. 25 In The *Sub 4 Minute Extra Mile* Series

ISBN: 978-1479389926

by **Ted Ciuba**

© MMXII PTIPTrust, *all rights reserved*

No part of this publication may be reproduced or transmitted in any form or by any means, mechanical or electronic, including photocopying and recording, or by any information storage and retrieval system, without permission in writing from author or publisher.

www.ThinkRich.com

info@ehaste.com

Parthenon Marketing Inc
2400 Crestmoor Rd #36
Nashville TN 37215   USA

Orders & Enrollments

+1-877- *4 RICHES*

***

phone +1-615-662-3169

OBLIGATORY LEGAL NOTICES: While consistent attempts have been made to authenticate information provided in this publication and to render it to high journalistic standards, neither the Author, Publisher, nor any speaker or participant makes any claims, promises, or guarantees about the accuracy, completeness, or adequacy of the information contained in this book or related products or linked to or referred to. You should assume we make money every time we refer a product; we may not, but assume so and you'll never be wrong. We make a profit on everything we do, as our highest purpose is to benefit all humanity. We do not assume, and hereby specifically disclaim, any responsibility for errors, omissions, contrary interpretation, or any other matter related to the subject matter and its rendering herein. Common sense obtains motivational writing has an element of faction to it. We make no warrants, guarantees, or representations regarding the use, matter, currentness, accuracy, completeness, adequacy, reliability, etc. of this work and all works associated with it. This is the only warrant of any kind, either express or implied; no oral or written information or advice given by us shall create a warranty or in any way increase the scope of this warranty, and you may not rely on such information or advice to do so. All statements are made relying on sources believed to be reliable. Any income or earnings claims made are for illustrative purposes only, and are believed to be true, but were not verified. *Your results will vary.*

Any perceived slights of specific persons, peoples, or organizations are unintentional, and if so indicated, will be amended in products going forward.

Products sold "as is" "with all faults" without warranties of any kind, either express or implied, including, but not limited to, the implied warranties of merchantability and fitness for a particular purpose. Under every circumstance, publisher's total liability is a refund of the purchase price. We are totally independent, and no reference, quote, case study, story, etc should in any way be construed as an indication our positions, words, actions, products are in any way authorized by, associated with, endorsed by, or sponsored by any outside entity. Any reference to "Think And Grow Rich" is by necessity in referring to the book title. THINK AND GROW RICH® is the registered trademark and property of the Napoleon Hill Foundation.

The purchaser or reader of this publication assumes full responsibility for the use of these materials and information, including adherence to all applicable laws and regulations, federal, state, and local, governing professional licensing, business practices, advertising, and all other aspects of doing business in the United States or any other jurisdiction in the world. Each individual's success depends on his or her background, dedication, desire and motivation. As shared in this book, though the qualifications to get in the game are so low as to be nearly universally available, getting rich always requires work, & could involve luck. Not to mention, everyone defines rich in their unique way. Right to make changes reserved. Author and Publisher assume NO RESPONSIBILITY or liability whatsoever on the behalf of any purchaser or reader of these information materials. The site of all actions pertaining in any way to these products or philosophies is Nashville, Tennessee, Davidson County USA. If you can't accept these terms, you do not have to participate in this offer.

Ted Ciuba is also the author of the incredible modernization and empowerment of Napoleon Hill's success classic, *Think & Grow Rich!*

Ted Ciuba

Quantum Business Acceleration Headcoach
Author of Sub 4 Minute Extra Mile Series

Tamara Doris

T.J. Rohleder

"This is **more than just a revamp with modern examples** - it radically transforms the vision by adding new gender, cross-cultural and international issues to the mix, including new material to include both science and genetics, as in the Quantum reality of accelerating income and wealth.

An excellent re-do of a classic financial inspirational guide."

"The writing is so much more applicable and understandable that I am literally forcing my friends, colleagues, and mastermind members to get their copies now! Every page fills me with passion and revs me up!"

"I picked up Ted's book -- AND I WAS SHOCKED AND AMAZED! I sat there and began going through it... and all of a sudden looked up and over 3 hours had gone by!!! I quickly read it from cover to cover within 2 days and then turned around and did it again! Ted has done a truly amazing thing by totally re-writing this powerful classic. Every entrepreneur and business owner simply MUST have Ted's book!"

www.ThinkRich.com/book

"You Are Closer To A Million Dollar$ Than You Now Dream!"

This is the modernized, quantum empowered version of Napoleon Hill's success classic, *Think And Grow Rich!*

#1 Best-Seller

An instruction manual to *consciously* direct the Quantum universe to manifest your positive desires."

Napoleon Hill Overlooks **Ted Ciuba**

Physical, Kindle. iStore

Are you ready for breakthrough progress overnight?!

- ➢ Engage with *The New Think And Grow Rich* - empower yourself! Start exactly where you are - no experience, no education, no cash required! Discover how to…
- ➢ Trigger the *self-fulfilling prophecy* and the *law of attraction*!
- ➢ Apply the insights of the secret "combination" to work for your immediate, easy success
- ➢ Direct the Quantum universe to deliver success
- ➢ Unleash that powerful "HoloMagic c2 factor" to accomplish your pursuits in a fraction of the time, with only a quanta of the effort

Mark Whyborn,
UK

*"I have read **The New Think And Grow Rich** and there is a **HUGE improvement** (so much more insight) in the new updated version!*

Once you learn the formula to riches, you can apply it to accelerate your income into the stratosphere!

Order now, for you, your company & your loved ones.

www.ThinkRich.com/book

Additional Sub 4 Minute Extra Mile Volumes Available!

Create Your Life By Design: Volume 1 in the Sub 4 Min
$7.95 Paperback

Know Your Purpose, Embrace Adventure: Vol. 2 In The
$7.95 Paperback

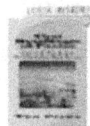

That HoloMagic c2 Factor: Vol. 3 In The Sub 4 Minute Ex
$7.95 Paperback

Create Your Life By Design (The Sub 4 Minute Extra Mi
$0.00 Prime Members
$2.99 Kindle Purchase

His New Business Called Him On The Phone: Vol. 10 In
$7.95 Paperback

> Check out the entire line of training sessions in The *Sub 4 Minute Extra Mile* Series!

http://ThinkRich.com/sub4min

**Full details on each title!
Complete your collection!
Give a meaningful gift!**

**While you're there, please REVIEW
And LIKE this volume ☺**

Table Of Contents

There's More Than Brain Entrainment Today 7
He Preferred To Pay Forty Thousand Dollars Rather Than Fly For Free ... 11
Ask The Question From A Totally Different Viewpoint 13
It's Never Living We Should Fear 15
I Just Saved Myself From Having A Grudge Against That Guy 17
Savor the Sweetness Of A Moment's Rain 19
Even Shakespeare Spoke Of The Mind-Environment Connection 23
Time In The HoloMagic Quantum Universe 25
Evidence Of Spelling Error Points To Mind-Environment Connection 27
It Will Always Be *This* Time 29
Any Time I've Ever Left Something Undone It's Never Got Done 31
The Not-Too-Symbolic Letting Go 35
It's Not All About Money, Crying In The Ecstasy 37
From Darkness To Light, The More Freedom You Enjoy 39
Eternity Happens In The Moment 41
Prepare Today For The Inevitable Tomorrow 43
Education Continues Forever-Learning Enough In An Hour 47
You Can Change That If You'll Make A Note 49
You Can't Win Trying Not To Lose 51

Vol. 25 In *The Sub 4 Minute Extra Mile* Series

IT WILL ALWAYS BE THIS TIME

by

Dr. Ted Ciuba

Introduction: It Takes So Little To Excel

As an achiever, would you agree with me that you must go the extra mile? *I thought so...*

Surely you know if you do what average people do, you'll get the same kind of average results they do. And something tells me you're a cut above that!

And it's actually quite easy to stand out, because most people wouldn't dream of going the extra mile. But for you and me, while, yes, it takes something extra, yes, it takes drive and discipline.... The amazing thing is, it takes so *little* to excel!

Roger Bannister
Runs Sub 4 Minute Mile

After all, it's called the extra *mile*, not the extra *100 miles!*

Be that as it may, we're talking about the positive rewards that come to you in any economy by going the extra mile.

It was Roger Bannister who defied and redefined history by running the sub 4 minute mile.

And the amazing thing is that Bannister did NOT spend the countless hours and hours practicing that conventional training would guide him to. He gave it what he could... In his busy pre-med Oxford schedule he took a mere 30 minutes out of his daily lunch hour to train and run. And with that he set a world record that had towered 3,000 years!

He ushered in a new era of possibility. Though no one had *ever* broken it, within 2 1/2 years time of Bannister's record-breaking,

Surf www.ThinkRich.com * Quantum Business Acceleration, $197 value gift *FREE*

seemingly unachievable sub 4 minute mile, 18 others were doing it.

And how did he do it?... It wasn't a function of *time*. Conventional sports training encompasses hours on an almost daily basis, not 30 minutes!!

It was *intention*. Roger Bannister, in the short, focused, regular, intense, intended few minutes per day he wrested from his busy Oxford pre-med studies was throwing himself into the sport. He gave it everything he could, as an additional interest and pursuit in his life...

You see, when Roger Bannister suffered the ignominious defeat of coming in 5th place in the 1952 Olympics, right then and there, he determined to be the first human to run the sub 4 minute mile!

It was just a "thought". It's just another instance and undisputable illustration, my friend, of the power of intention powered by determination.

Moments before 6 pm on 6 May 1954, he takes a breath of vision and determination. He feels it! He confides to his pacemakers "The sub 4 minute attempt is on!"

Short moments later the shot is fired... The runners are off!! Roger Bannister breaks the string at the end of the mile in 3 minutes, 59 seconds, and 4/10's, trailblazing into the sub 4 minute mile age!

Recognition Point!! - This was NOT an unintended event! Recognition point!! Little efforts, little accomplishments - short, focused, regular, intense, intended training sessions - gear into colossal events!

Visit HoloMagic.com for $297 in free empowerment gifts

Also note how little it takes to stand waaay beyond the competition! Roger Bannister redefined history in one evening... And he did it only with the razor's edge of difference, 1/10 of a second over 1/2 of a second!!!

This didn't happen by circumstance... Roger Bannister didn't "drift" over the finish line into the annals of history... It was the thing he geared all his intentions to accomplish, even though he didn't spend hours and hours a day in the quest to achieve it.

Which gives rise to the name of this series, The *Sub 4 Minute Extra Mile* Series...

Now you, honoring Roger Bannister's history-setting accomplishments and methods, can make the same kind of history-breaking progress in sub 4 minutes a day! Defy the status quo in short, focused, regular, intense, intended training sessions and redefine what's possible and what you accomplish!

NOTES

Item /passage /page	Insight	Action

THERE'S MORE THAN BRAIN ENTRAINMENT TODAY

In nature, as in physics, there's a phenomenon known as *entrainment*. It's like when a man brings 400 grandfather clocks into a room and it's chaotic because they're all doing their own thing. But you give it a few days or weeks, and they all tick, tick, tick in rhythm.

We do the same thing in personal development and personal achievement, in the programs where there are meditative trancelike things, hypnotic kinds of things. *Entrainment*. We play a music that matches what would be good for the human mind to be productive and to facilitate access to higher abilities, and we have *superlearning*.

Now, I have no issues with *entrainment*, often called *brain entrainment*. It's good. This thing has been around for a while. At one time it was breakthrough technology.

Which points to the issues I have, being, while brainwave entrainment is not obsolete, it is old technology. It's time to embrace it and move on, not to keep featuring it like it's a new thing.

There's a new system called *neurosynergist sound technology*®. It's way advanced.

Consider it like this... True, the *principles* of flight have never changed since we took off at Kitty Hawk. But don't you think an F-16 fighter jet is a *lot* more sophisticated than the Wright brothers' cloth wing airplane?

So what happened is, brainwave entrainment hasn't gone bad—but there's so much more that can happen now. See, brainwave entrainment is a rhythm. But there are sounds, frequencies, and tones that, with the passage of time, we've

Surf www.ThinkRich.com * Quantum Business Acceleration, $197 value gift *FREE*

discovered facilitate profound, self-determining, spiritual states of power.

Now, I'm not even going to go into what part *neuro-linguistic programming* (NLP) plays in the experience of the adoption of change at the subconscious level... And how it works in sub-audible messages – sub-audible to the *ears,* not to the *subconscious mind* - because that's also part of it, too.

There's different affirmations spoken in both ears at the same time. In different persons – it dazzles the mind and sets new neurons firing.

This is part of the technology.

I'm talking about the science of sound right now.

So what is neurosynergist sound technology®?

Let me just give you a few ideas. For example, there's a woman and a man, that's the yin and the yang, masculine and feminine into waves rolling out on the nighttime beach blend into a mother's heartbeat in the womb that wakes you to the positive primal rhythms of life...

When you put that on an audio program or video program, it wakes up certain energies, which in turn causes the breakup of old stuck systems that no longer serve you.

Sparkling waters mean something to the human animal, you know that. When they flow over the crevices of the prepared and opened subconscious mind directly, they bring eternity into the moment. That develops into psychological poise and balance as you navigate through the real world.

There's the "sound thrower," which throws sound around, around, around, around, around, around and it enchants. It's a novel thing that enchants you. That loosens the resistance your subconscious mind might otherwise have, and gives the seeds of change tossed on the ground the chance to sprout and take hold...

The spring call of morning birds is shown to foster spectacular points of change.

And you're led up and down the brainwave frequencies – *beta, alpha, theta, delta* blended into *gamma*... All by different sounds and frequencies. This makes you a whole, integrated person, with almost superhuman powers of perception.

Put succinctly, this tends to make you a person who comprehends cause and effect in the Universe, a Higher Power, love to family and service to society, and turns it on to achieve any worthy goal you and your invisible counselors decide upon...

There are new scientific marvels coming out of the neuroscience labs at the great universities...

The chirping of crickets, for instance, bows the strings of your reticular activating system, so you become hyper aware of the synchronicities and opportunities you encounter in your ordinary passage through business and life– that are usually overlooked completely unawares.

The calls of whales and dolphins engage your emotions and open your higher consciousness... They etch neural grooves in your reticular activating system so you ONLY notice the things that fast track you to wealth...

Do you know the sun makes a sound you can hear if you compress it with computer technology? *That's* in this technology! These waves develop the neural pathways that connect the cycles, the seasons, and business growth and your abilities to create residual income.

Surf www.ThinkRich.com * Quantum Business Acceleration, $197 value gift *FREE*

Do you know the stars make some of those same sounds, too? There's even, in this neurosynergist sound technology®, the computer-generated sound of interstellar space. Believe it! This interstellar waves made audible align you to Natural Law at sublime levels.

What are waves? That's what it all is, right?

You are a star being. Don't let your local experience becloud the true facts... Every single thing in your life will transform in the flash you accept that reality. Where better to facilitate that transformation than amongst the stars?

All these things, and many more, are brought into neurosynergist sound technology® in a big way. This is new technology, brainwave entrainment is just one little aspect of it.

I could go on and on—there's more. You're just getting the idea that we need to go beyond brainwave entrainment now, to go into the next generation of personal development change.

HE PREFERRED TO PAY FORTY THOUSAND DOLLARS RATHER THAN FLY FOR FREE

He preferred to pay $40,000, rather than fly for free.

I know it sounds like a preposterous thing. I'm talking about a multi-millionaire businessman. I'm not going to identify the person now—even though, of course, I'm speaking about a specific one.

But $40,000—that's the price of a direct flight for him to fly his jet from his home base to Seattle, Washington. Well, that's not that bad, but of course that doesn't include all the upkeep. That's the price of a flight, not the price of the plane, the insurance, the pilot's salary, the payments, etcetera.

But he preferred to pay that $40,000 than to fly for free, because it meant a whole lot of time saving, of efficiency, of movement. He can cover more ground is less time. It's just like getting a better car. You *enjoy* the process of driving in a good car; you endure it in a poor car.

And so, bottom line, it was worth $40,000 to him. It was the payoff of only one student coming into one of his upper-end programs—just one! Economics even made it reasonable.

But you know how times can change.

Did you hear there's a recession going on? I've seen him, lately, flying coach, and hey, he'll be the first to say, "It costs $40,000 versus $560," or, truth be told, absolutely zero—free—because at this time, we have frequent flyer rewards programs with the airlines.

In other words, he's running his business through his credit cards. Even though he pays them off every month, he's using those free frequent flyer rewards miles. Somebody's making

Surf www.ThinkRich.com * Quantum Business Acceleration, $197 value gift *FREE*

money, that's why they're doing this, right? They're giving him miles.

He has so many miles he could fly around the world 14 times before he even needed to check into his balance. For him, airline flight *is* free. *Even* if we mention a normal price, you do the math. He says, "I'm being economical, I'm helping our company". And times *have* changed.

When the economy calls us to pull in our belt, all we do is pull in our belt. That's it.

Sure, money is flowing less freely, and even, some would say, less recklessly... And we keep making money, we keep finding new ways to make money, we really snort out those who are currently making money and see what we can do to model, mimic, and adapt from them.

Inability to change is a recipe for extinction. Flexibility is key. In all things.

And it'll come back to a time again when, if you prefer, you'll pay the $40,000 rather than take the free flight, because that's what you prefer and it serves you better.

But for today...

ASK THE QUESTION FROM A TOTALLY DIFFERENT VIEWPOINT

There's many nuances to achieving success. Some of them are just unexamined, uncaught. For instance, I was with a small group the other day and we were launching a project. And to launch a project you've got to do a little bit of work - you've got to design it, you have to acquire and organize it, you have to capture and produce it, you've got a website to build and make operational, copy to write and sundry necessary items. Then you start the marketing, tracking every ad.

These are all things akin to sharpening the ax when you have a tree to fell.

All the public sees is flash and thunder when the tree comes crashing down, but there's a lot of work that goes on behind that.

And someone's asking, "Well, should we really design to go forward with this?"

I'm thinking, "Hold on, where did this come from?"

There's two things. Number one, we teach, we recommend, we advise, you always test small, roll out large. So looking for a self-funding, affordable test at the beginning is not an indication of where we're going. That's good sound business.

Number two ... We can get so caught up *doing* things we forget *why* we're doing them. To break that mental log jam, sometimes if we'll ask the absolute reverse of the question we're stuck on, that can make the answer obvious.

For instance, take that same kind of question, which effectively asks, "Should we go ahead and push forward on this and develop it and make it become all it can be if it goes?"

Surf www.ThinkRich.com * Quantum Business Acceleration, $197 value gift *FREE*

Turn that whole question around and ask, "Can you think of a good reason, if this thing takes off like we suspect it will, we should hold back?" That asks if we should satisfy ourselves with a portion of the profit we can earn. If we should only help a meager amount of people instead of scaling up. Is that what we should do?

And then the answer, when you turn the question totally around, can be so obvious. That's the whole thing, by the way, about the mastermind. That's the idea behind brainstorming and creative thinking, giving other viewpoints and experience a place to be heard and a chance to kick in.

There you have it, one handy device I use that helps me break the log jam in my mind and let the river flow. Ask the question from a totally different viewpoint.

It's Never Living We Should Fear

It is not *dying* we should fear; it is *never living* we should fear. You see, we have a choice, we have an option. We have a life loaned to us. We already *know* we'll die. And you can debate about how or when, but unfortunately or not, we can't know those aspects of the certain fact.

When and how we'll die is speculation. That we'll die is certain.

I'm not certain that's unfortunate. I mean, I would hate to think I had six days, and everything I had to do had to be done within six days. Even though I may die in the next moment. Even though I'm planning on living decades more... There's a peace about living in the illusion life will go on and on...

On the other hand, you do have a set number of days...and everything you want to do, wish to do, could do, would like to do, want to experience, want to leave behind is to be done during this short period of time you have.

It was Michelangelo who said,

> The greater danger for most of us lies not in setting our aim too high and falling short; but in setting our aim too low, and achieving our mark.

Don't fear dying—fear never having lived. Write that book, ask that person out on a date, encourage your son or daughter, put them through the school you don't think you can afford, walk out on faith. Whatever it is, my friend, it's up to you.

You may die before you finish the task, it's true. But you probably won't, if you get right to it. But even if you do, at least you died striving, working, contributing.

I am reminded of the immortal words of Odysseus, rendered by Lord Alfred Tennyson,

Surf www.ThinkRich.com * Quantum Business Acceleration, $197 value gift *FREE*

> Death closes all; but something ere the end,
>
> Some work of noble note, may yet be done,
>
> Not unbecoming men that strove with Gods.

You have one choice, one chance only. There is no perfection. You're going to look back, and what do you want to look back on? A life of daring adventure, a life of going for it? A life of experience—or a life where you played it safe all the time, never took any risks, never enjoyed any bravado, and never really *had* a life?

I Just Saved Myself From Having A Grudge Against That Guy

I just saved myself from having a grudge against this guy. Look, this is funny I know, but I'm being honest.

I went out to lunch, ran by a salad bar, and snatched a small group of groceries, right? I'm checking out, in a run back to the office. The clerk puts my salad, in a flimsy plastic container, into a grocery sack. And he puts a couple apples on top of it. An unthinking act. A throws some grapes over the lip of the bag on top of the flimsy container. And he's about to throw something else and I said, "STOP!! Please, that's enough!"

Because I knew what was going to happen.

He didn't, he wasn't working with consciousness and awareness, he didn't care about his job, he just had to do something to get paid. But he was about to crush my little plastic salad and I'd get to the office and have nothing. So, I stopped him.

Now, it's not the end of the world, it's not hardly anything, except for it is a true fact that illustrates we can intervene in so many big and little ways. I would've had a grudge against that guy. I wouldn't have gone to his supervisor, and I wouldn't have gone and told him off. I see people do those kinds of things all the time, and it's crazy. I just never would've thought much of him and I would've avoided him.

Now, I didn't have those negative feelings.

What?! I could've had a grudge against that guy!

NOTES

Item /passage /page	Insight	Action

SAVOR THE SWEETNESS OF A MOMENT'S RAIN

The immigration officer at Immigration and Naturalization Service (INS) Miami was doing his job, asking me the usual interrogating questions: "How long have you been there?" "What was the purpose of your trip?"

They have the intelligence already for most of the questions, they track, sort, sift, classify, and have ready almost everything you do. It would be Hitler's dream, I'm sure. Welcome to the technoconnected modern world. He's got the answers already on his screen, so, could I dare answer wrong?

And he asked, "Have you ever been to Panamá before?"

I said, "Man, very, very often."

And of course, I am aware Panamá has an unjustly earned appellation as one of the rogue regimes—though that's just my opinion, because I'm not involved in the circles that see it that way. This is a great way for the politicians to discount the country and then rally support... I could go on, but I won't.

I'm involved. I've got a wife and a child there. So after all the interrogation's over, the guy just kind of smiles, gets human, and he says, "You're a lucky man." And it is true.

I live in two countries. But here's what I want to tell you: I see my experience in Panamá as a metaphor for the way we should live in life. Let me make it real simple for you. My work is in the U.S. I am a U.S. citizen. My love and my home life are in Panamá. I spend most of my time in the U.S., so we spend most of our time separated.

Now what that does for us is that when we're together, we cherish every moment.

We go out to a resort, we go out to the beach, we do things, we don't just vegetate. We go out to eat a lot—if not every night,

Surf www.ThinkRich.com * Quantum Business Acceleration, $197 value gift *FREE*

it's more often than every other night, and if you put it together with the lunches we're able to fit in, do we go out to eat once a day? Yes, we absolutely do.

We're doing things together. We're going to the park at dawn, before the work day starts. We're going weekends with the family to Amador to share love and adventure of the wholesome type with others in a festive environment.

It's the sweetness of a moment's rain coupled with the awareness the moment to enjoy it is now.

In the same way, the moment to accomplish is now, because we also know, because we've been in this environment, there are times of desert and times of no fruit. And it's the same way we cherish every moment we're together because we're apart so much. In the midst of the desert of separation our reunions are visits to the oasis. Ah, the sweetness of a moment's rain!

Think of life in the same way. We come into this little moment of eternity streaking on the move.

Eternity isn't going to begin after we die. That would make the definition of eternity faulty. *Wake up. We*'re living in eternity. Already. We're participants. Quantum physicists tell us every unit of creation, at whatever level has consciousness.

We're what this section of eternity does eternally. We're just streaks of light in the endless round of constant creation and destruction, the eternal cycle of life. Eternity began an eternal number of years before, and continues an eternal number of years past.

But we? We find ourselves here this moment, and it's like me going to Panamá to be with my girls.

We've got just a brief period of time and we've got to do everything we can. For us it's to love every person, to respect every person, to contribute, to make as much money as suits our needs and ambitions, take care of our family, and to enjoy the moment. We are put here to enjoy—not in the glutton sense, but in the sense of the same way the birds and the butterflies and the young fish enjoy themselves in the sweetness of a moment's rain.

Yes, my friend, I wish to you that you cherish the brief moments of awareness you may enjoy in this huge big thing they call eternity as you savor the sweetness of a moment's rain.

Surf www.ThinkRich.com * Quantum Business Acceleration, $197 value gift *FREE*

NOTES

Item /passage /page	Insight	Action

EVEN SHAKESPEARE SPOKE OF THE MIND-ENVIRONMENT CONNECTION

>Our lives are our gardens,
>
>our wills are our gardeners.

William Shakespeare said that.

Look between the lines, read between the lines... "Our lives are our gardens, our wills are our gardeners." He's talking about the *mind-environment connection*, a quantum concept well known by various intelligent, inspired individuals throughout the eons of time.

The mind-environment connection... As we *think*, as you *think*... The proper order is *think* and *grow rich*... Outer results are the manifestation, the visualization, the actualization, the realization of who we are inside. The choices we've made. The values we live by.

"Our wills are our gardeners." As you *think*. If you think sloppy, you live sloppy. If you think with forethought and vision, you have a life, a purpose, and you are accomplishing throughout the career of your life that which you are wanting to do.

The mind-environment connection. It keeps showing up in inspired places, time and time. It *is* time you take it to heart and realize you'd *better* get your thinking under control, into action. If you're lagging behind right now don't let that worry you, because all it takes is a decision to change.

It takes a decision to become a completely different person. If you will decide with a will which cuts off all alternatives, decide with a commitment to do what it takes to make it happen, in this moment you begin planting new seeds, tending new plants which

Surf www.ThinkRich.com * Quantum Business Acceleration, $197 value gift *FREE*

certainly will harvest into new fruit and circumstance in their appropriate hour.

You can grasp this concept. It's not new. Even Shakespeare spoke of the *mind-environment connection*. What we see around us is a panorama of our choices.

"Our lives are our gardens." They're what we've created. The life force, as long as we're living, expresses through us. Will it be a well tended garden, something we're proud of? Will it be weeds and trash?

> Our lives are our gardens,
>
> our wills are our gardeners.
>
> - William Shakespeare

In modern language for you and me, that says the *mind-environment connection*.

Tend your mind.

TIME IN THE HOLOMAGIC QUANTUM UNIVERSE

It is *noooot* time that determines how rapidly or how far you achieve your goals.

I like to tell the story about Roger Bannister. Now you talk about someone takin' on something big, somethin' that nobody in the *world* could do, nobody in the world had *ever* done!! And it was clear - everybody knew that, and the medical establishment even warned - it would be dangerous to the health and life of any individual who even *attempted* to run the sub-4 minute mile.

Remember we're saying it's not *time*. It's *intention,* and there is no better case study than Roger Bannister, who didn't participate in the 1948 Olympics, a bad choice he repented during opening ceremonies.

He immediately started preparing to go to the '52 Olympics. He went, and he came in 5th place in his event.

And that was as bad as it gets. Burning in shame, he determined right then and there to do what no human had ever done before, to run the sub-4 minute mile.

Only one thing stood in his way. He was a busy pre-med student with sooo little time. And he could not devote himself to the 4-6 hours per day expected training regimen.

He gave it what he *could*, 30 minutes a day. He had a lunch hour in his busy pre-med Oxford University schedule. Majoring in neuroscience!

So he had an hour free at lunch every day. He gave 30 minutes of that hour to practice - 30 minutes, a mere 30 minutes! He had to save the rest of the time to shower, cool down, eat his lunch and do a little bit of socializing.

Surf www.ThinkRich.com * Quantum Business Acceleration, $197 value gift *FREE*

And the day he ran that sub-4 minute mile, 6 May 1954, some 60 seconds from the beginning shot, he advised his pacemaker, "The sub-4 minute attempt is on."

You see, he called it, just like you'd call a pool ball going into the corner pocket. This didn't happen by accident. I don't know why that isn't made more notice of. Of course, I always make a lot of it myself. It was an *intended* thing, something nobody could do. How big is that?

Nobody had ever done it, in thousands of years of trying. Remember, the Olympics come from *Ancient* Greece. That record had stood.

And then comes one man motivated to the point of determination. Roger Bannister defied and re-defined human possibility.

He ushered in a new era of possibility. Though no one had *ever* broken it previously, within 2 1/2 years time of Bannister's record-breaking sub 4 minute mile, 18 others were doing it. Today a sub-4 minute mile is a qualifier to even be considered serious.

It was not the quantity of time he put to his dream, no, not in this holomagic, quantum universe. It was the *intention* with which he invested the little time he did dedicate to it.

EVIDENCE OF SPELLING ERROR POINTS BACK TO MIND-ENVIRONMENT CONNECTION

When you make something as simple as a spelling error in a letter you're writing... Let's consider that for a moment. We look at the page. Where was the error created? Was the error created on the page? Of course not! The page shows the result, the page is an environment, a medium that takes the impress the fingers give it.

Now, we're assuming the machine's working right, of course, because if you found a key that was always typing the wrong letter that would indeed be a different story and the error would be in the machine.

So we're eliminating the machine right now. And is the error in the finger? We've got a spelling error. It was the finger that typed the letter on the page. The error is not on the page - that's the result, that's the medium. The error surely isn't in the finger, either. The finger was only a medium of transmission – it has no thinking capacity on its own, does it?

Would you agree with me, the error for what shows up on the page, originated in the mind? This is a sterling illustration of the *mind-environment connection*. Everything in your life is a *result*, you live in *results*.

What you do, how you act, is going to be a cause for a future result, another result. And you can change, you can re-steer.

If you're going down this road, the issue is not in the vehicle you're in, or the steering wheel, though it's going down that road. The issue is in the mind. The environment simply reflects what the mind holds within it. Once you change your mind you can, and in fact you *do* steer the car to a different environment.

Surf www.ThinkRich.com * Quantum Business Acceleration, $197 value gift *FREE*

And that's how easy it can be, but we do need to do some reinforcement to make sure it's there and programmed, re-programmed. Once you change your mind you can re-steer that car. You've *decided*, *YOU* have decided. And what you see about you is the result of the decisions and the mind you apply.

The classic *mind-environment connection*.

It Will Always Be *This* Time

The more conscious we are, the better we create it. The *less* conscious we are, the worse it comes out—as an individual, as a family, as a couple, a company or a country - whatever it is.

The future is unformed; the observer affects the observed. The future is full of endless possibilities from which you choose... Every step you takes you in a certain direction.

The future and all that comes in it— society, opportunity, your abilities, your efforts—is both affected by and affecting the world. And governments run their countries the same way you can run your life. There *are* forces.

Today is the time, today is the only time we ever have, ever *will* have. We will be judged by what we do at *this* time. We will *be* what we create at this time.

That's what this *endless present* the mystics speak of means... While we're creating the future, it will always be *this time*. There is no other time to take action, to enjoy life, to share time with those you love, to contribute, to get conscious in unraveling ongoing creation.

And when we arrive in the future, we will be in the present. It can and should be the progressive present we build with our strategic, beneficial thoughts and actions.

Co-create your future for yourself, your family, your friends, your company, your community, society, your country, and the world.

It starts by deciding to make something of the chance you've got.

Surf www.ThinkRich.com * Quantum Business Acceleration, $197 value gift *FREE*

Notes

Item /passage /page	Insight	Action

ANY TIME I'VE EVER LEFT SOMETHING UNDONE IT'S NEVER GOT DONE

What are your biggest goals, dreams and ambitions? What is it that you *really* want to do? You may be involved in doing it; or you may not have decided to pay the price and picked up the gauntlet yet.

You want to find the answer and throw yourself emotionally involved with it. What *will* be your contribution on Earth, as Napoleon Hill calls it, your definite chief aim?

Now, you've got to be realistic, of course. If you're 85 years old, you're not going to become another Elvis Presley. But then again, you don't have to be Elvis Presley to make a huge and significant contribution to the world. Grandma Moses didn't even paint her first painting till she was in her 70's. She had an entire career ahead of her. She painted up to her very last days. She painted, as she did every day, on her 101st birthday.

Here's the thing—step up your game. Past occupations are past. Excuses don't count. You DO have to get into focused action.

Are you currently in motion accomplishing your definite chief aim in life? Are you actually *doing* something? Have you gotten conscious and created a plan, have you had others look at the plan, have you bounced it off them, listened to advice? This is not the one-night brainstorm of a guy who has too many beers, you know, this is your life!

And here's what we both know... Time is brief, very brief. You never get a chance to come back and do it again. Whatever you want to be known for, whether it's raising that beautiful family, or building that magnificent industry, or being the first civilian to

Surf www.ThinkRich.com * Quantum Business Acceleration, $197 value gift *FREE*

climb the seven highest peaks of the world... Whatever it is, the way you do it is *right now*.

Time is so brief you'll never have another opportunity. It occurs to me, in my own career... I have been writing since I was seven years old. I knew when I was seven, in the second grade, sitting in the back, from Mrs. Matlock's teacher's position, to the right of the classroom—not the very last row, but pretty close... It was there, with my desktop open and paper in my hand -

I popped into an alternate reality – don't even know what happened in the classroom, but when I returned to normal consciousness, all was progressing tranquilly along just fine as I'd left it some magical second without time...

It seemed soooo right and logical at once... A *brilliant* discovery I made in that interdimensional moment... And I exclaimed up with delight, "I know, I'll be an author!"

I'd discovered the treasure of my life!

I knew I wanted to be an author. And through many ventures coming up the way, I have the experience now of decades of being an author.

And you know, any time I've ever left anything unsaid, it's never been said. No matter how noble the sentiment, no matter how beneficial it can be, at any time... This is true with childish juvenile stuff, this is true in my early 20's when I was writing poetry to girls, this is true in my marketing career, this is true in the Sub4Minute Extra Mile series of articles that is so dear to my current heart.

Any time I've ever left anything unsaid, it's never been said. Any time I've ever left something undone, it has never gotten done. You only get one chance at life, but gears within gears – you only get one chance at each of the epochs of life, too. Same thing for the sub epochs...

Visit HoloMagic.com for $297 in free empowerment gifts

Imagine it; at 22, I *felt* the poetry I was writing for those sexy little young things. Could you imagine me feeling the same way now, past 60, with the same passion, with the same willingness to dedicate endless hours of time to getting it right, to getting it said, to being creative?

No. That epoch and those activities are gone. Respectfully, whatever passions I had then, my interests and energies are other wheres now. You can't go back.

Whatever epic you have at hand, that you want to create. Do it now, because this epoch will be gone shortly, also.

NOTES

Item /passage /page	Insight	Action

THE NOT-TOO-SYMBOLIC LETTING GO

It's happening in my professional career, too, but I've never seen such a clear illustration of it as I did tonight - in my personal life.

My daughter is engaged to a young man, and this is the first time I've met him. All that is very fine and good, and we had a dinner together. He seems to be a fine gentleman. There has to be a first time. So what we do when we're parting?

Now, you've got to understand, my daughter and I have a history. I have been her "knight in shining armor" for thirty years.

I've been her knight in shining armor for all her life. I have been the one who opened her car door, I have been the one who tucked her in, and even as an adult when she didn't need it, I was the one who took her up to her door and got her securely in her car, and then I walked away.

Just a little bit of changing of the guard going on, I guess. This time, after this dinner, at a wonderful place, we had a wonderful time with this wonderful man, wonderful *everything*—we go up and there's just an instant of discomfort. It doesn't last too long because between us, since we understand each other so well—of course she would understand that.

But there was that instant of discomfort. And then, after we embraced, we let loose and I told her, "Okay, it's *your* knight who's going to open your car door tonight."

It's a letting-go. A forerunner of the symbolic ceremony in the wedding where the father gives the bride to her man. It's happening in real life.

I share today not a financial interest story but a human interest story.

Surf www.ThinkRich.com * Quantum Business Acceleration, $197 value gift *FREE*

Because this *will* come, or *has* come in your life, if the Gods grant you that blessing.

It's Not All About Money, Crying In The Ecstasy

Wow, it's been one emotional Sunday morning, I must say. It was just last night I met my prospective in-laws. My daughter is seriously involved with a man, and, of course, I don't know and you don't know how it'll turn out. But we're going through the motions right now, and it looks like it's going that way.

Well of course, that was something. I mean, this is my little girl—my little girl who's 30 years old. But it's like if you've ever seen the motion picture *Father of the Bride.* I look at her and I see her as three *weeks* old. You know, emotionally.

And then, there's my son, who gets educated, is involved with a woman. They move off to Shanghai, China and then they slip off while celebrating the Chinese New Year to Thailand and marry there. How romantic!

Just this morning I came running by the office. I've got a couple of extra hours before church... I make it that way, because I love what I'm doing. And there's a picture album of their wedding that just came in. The wedding was like two or three weeks ago, but the picture album just arrived.

I have to *suffer* through that. I mean, it's suffering in the emotion—it's crying in the ecstasy. I am so happy, I'm so *proud*.

And these are moments I affirm it is *not* all about money.

Since money is our medium of exchange, all of us are oriented and focused on money. It's a manner of measuring productivity. It's a way of comparing opportunities.

Money is a necessary in a long, happy, healthy, productive life... There's the old joke, "Money's not everything, but it's right up there with oxygen!"

Surf www.ThinkRich.com * Quantum Business Acceleration, $197 value gift *FREE*

And then we share moments of joy. Joy so often comes packaged with family.

There's only a very small group of individuals in all the world we share the family bond with... And life *is* better than it would be in the vacuum without that bond.

I wish it for you.

FROM DARKNESS TO LIGHT, THE MORE FREEDOM YOU ENJOY

We met through our professional affairs. He was one of those friends you like, you respect, and you hold at a distance. He spent many years as a P.I., a private investigator. And when I was with him, it's kind of like being with a person who's psychic— you're always afraid that they're reading your mind, or they're engaging your motives, or they're finding something in you and in your past that you wouldn't want them to know about.

This is true even when you don't normally feel like you're running or hiding. Catch my drift? Skeleton in the closet, that kind of stuff. So I never felt comfortable around him.

And he had a book—again, investigative arts, going against people, is not my bag I'll admit. But he had a book he wrote called *From Darkness Into Light: How To Find Out if Your Spouse is Cheating on You*.

That's another thing I didn't like, because, one, I don't catch the kind of spouses who *would* be cheating, and, two, that's a seedy side of life. Again, I'm not interested.

But, while the subject was not my bag, the title always intrigued me: *From Darkness Into Light*.

Now, why am I mentioning this? It's definitely a metaphor. What he was saying was, "We'll turn the light on this and we'll be able to see."

I thought of Michael Enlow just last night, may he rest in peace. I hadn't thought of him in some time. Why today?

The psychologists call it *association*. Last night I was setting up some audio equipment, and I was in a dimly-lit office, in candlelight. We had the ambiance thing going—and I couldn't

Surf www.ThinkRich.com * Quantum Business Acceleration, $197 value gift *FREE*

connect it. I couldn't see where the screw hole was, where it would connect.

So... I take it into the light. I flip on the light, move instantly from darkness into light. In a moment I had the solution I hadn't been able to find in minutes of fumbling.

Yes, there *is* a time to bring things from darkness into light. When we're looking for the details, we turn up the light figuratively, metaphorically—and sometimes physically, actually. From darkness into light: the path to knowledge, the path to action.

It applies on every level, in every stratosphere, in any dimension. The more you seek what the real players do, the more you understand, the more power you amass, and the more freedom you enjoy.

ETERNITY HAPPENS IN THE MOMENT

Eternity comes in the moment. Hey, I have just spent five almost brutal days, I mean we were working from early morning, which would be 8 or 9 officially, until late in the evening, which would be when we finish dinner around 10:00 pm. If you have a wrap-up drink with your comrades that can extend a little bit.

I'd been working hard - and you know I'm not complaining, I love it's my passion. But I got on a plane in Jacksonville, flying back to Nashville, thinking this was going to be a good opportunity to review my notes, to organize my strategy. And then "Tessa" sits down beside me.

I was in the window seat, there was a man in the aisle, we hadn't even acknowledged each other. And it was just a flash moment, you know how Southwest is, its open boarding. Just at the last moment, when the last woman comes in, sits down beside me.

She looked at me, so I greeted her. She said, "Oh, you're social!" Well, it wasn't that *I* was social, it was that *she* was social.

My plans for the moment went right out the door. Here we were, two strangers, two ships passing in the dark. And we began to talk, and we shared the things of our lives, we shared the things of our adventures. I mean she was going to a place about 120 miles from Nashville to visit her mother, who was sick.

We talked about metaphysics – she had been to Machu Pichu and to the Great Pyramid in Egypt. We talked about the world. We talked about Washington. It was just—it was like entertainment for me. It was like listening to a radio show and being engaged instead of just having clutter going on in the background.

Surf www.ThinkRich.com * Quantum Business Acceleration, $197 value gift *FREE*

It was a moment of freedom; it was a moment of joy. With a stranger, unexpected, un-asked for, but recognized and taken.

You see, eternity, the richness life has to offer, comes in many forms, and it always happens in the *moment*.

There's a reason why they say, *"Carpe diem!"* That's the Latin version from ancient imperial Rome. This is not new wisdom, though each human learns anew. In big things and in little, translated into English it says, *"Seize the day!"*

PREPARE TODAY FOR THE INEVITABLE TOMORROW

I had the extreme good fortune today of spending several hours with a young lady of 88 years of age. It was very interesting, and there's a message in this for you. The lady was, at times, perfectly lucid, could not be fooled. And at times, was foolish.

It serves as a good reminder the Gods have ordained the path we follow from the cradle to the grave.

And it is so true. I mean I thank God my daughter's now seven years old and she's a whole lot more reasonable and participative than she was when she was from two to three, when she thought the world was her oyster and should conform to her demands and outlook, etcetera, etcetera. Entirely normal.

This is exactly what I saw with this lady. Sometimes she couldn't be fooled; sometimes she *had* to be fooled. She doesn't like being alone, and at one point we were trying to get her to get in the car and go home, so one of the ladies said "Your daughter, Sinia, is coming to see you."

That sparked her eyes. She jumped up and she said "You're lying!" Now, all of this is happening in Spanish, but the language doesn't matter, she said, "You're lying! Is it true?" In other words, she knew it wasn't and she wanted it to be.

And when the lady, who was not willing to outright lie again and compound a sin, said, "I think so," this lady was lucid enough to go *BAM!* She sat right back down in her seat and wasn't about to move.

We're here talking about human potential and wealth development.. Spirituality is thrown in there, but its part and partial of human potential, right?

Surf www.ThinkRich.com * Quantum Business Acceleration, $197 value gift *FREE*

The pathway of our life traces a cosmic arc across the sky. Our life takes off with energy and fire and we rise up the arc only to decline on the other side as we glide into a disappearing landing.

We rise from the womb through babyhood, we rise through adolescence into adulthood, we take on the jobs and the times, we rise through middle age when and where we peak.

And then, having past the crest, we begin riding down the other side of the arc.

The human is a bit different than most earthlings, in that we have a mind we can use to reason and to calculate with. We live an arc. We use money, we consume resources. *Prepare.* That's the message, prepare today.

Think of investing and do it. *Think* of the value of regular investing over time in your income earning years. Calculate the value of different regular contributions compounded at different rates over time.

Get started with whatever you can. The amount you can put in is not nearly as important as the regularity and never taking it out. Stay open to finding ways to up your contributions as you go along, but get started today.

You must prepare for your future days, because there will come a time when you are feeble. That is, if the Gods bless you, there will come a time when you are not always lucid, when you go in and out of intelligence. It's the same in a dog and a cat, they're not as loveable when they're old as when they're young. They're not as energetic, they're not as creative, they're not so delightful. Neither will you be.

Prepare today for the inevitable tomorrow. Think, plan, put your plan into action, and maintain it with persistence so you can live and you can leave in dignity.

Visit HoloMagic.com for $297 in free empowerment gifts

And if you want to do something special, if you want to really see somebody light up, why don't you buy one of these elderly ladies on the failing edge of their life a simple single red rose? See what you can do for her.

NOTES

Item /passage /page	Insight	Action

EDUCATION CONTINUES FOREVER-LEARNING ENOUGH IN AN HOUR

I just checked into the Marriott Hotel in Orlando, Florida for a conference. Real work, where we're dressed up and speaking from the stage begins tomorrow. And when I was on the plane I wanted to be brought up to speed on *press releases*. I've never written any deal of press releases. I've taken a stab at it once or twice, so I needed to get some education.

Got it!

Therein is the point of my conversation... An hour, maybe 90-minutes at most, and now I have the big vision of that field. I have places in mind, I'm using the internet where I can go and place some free. There are other placements I can pay for. I've analyzed the benefits. I've got familiar with the structure and rhythm of an efficient press release. I've read about 12 of them; I printed them off right before I left. For you who have those same interests, the best resource site is www.PRWeb.com

And so, here you are... Let's call it a long hour, and I have become competent to take some action in a new field. That's the point, how easy it is to stay abreast, how easy it is to go into a new field. Education is not something that ended when we got our high school diplomas, or if you want to go one level above that, when we got our college degrees. No, education continues forever in this fast moving world.

It's especially relevant to every professional in today's cyber-connected world.

The fact is the world, and knowledge, and technology, and science ,and art, and every form of human endeavor is exploding on every front. And in fact, you'd *better* be staying young and nimble, staying abreast of what's going on, because if you don't, just trying to stand still, you're going backwards compared to the rapid forward progress others are embracing.

This isn't your competitors, the stars, or just plain bad luck, you're the one holding yourself back. Your competitors are managing to do it.

And the good news is, with a little bit of dedicated time and focus you can conquer a new field real quick, real easy.

These are your human capacities. It is the uniqueness of the human *mind* which makes the human animal different than all other animals.

Use it!

You Can Change That If You'll Make A Note

Keep note cards, and a pen handy at all times. Keep a digital voice recorder, and a video recorder (which can double as a voice recorder) with you so that anytime you have a brilliant idea, you can catch it. Hey, one of my preferred forms of exercising is running in a national park—and I even take a pen and note cards with me there.

Especially there! Coming with a head full of the current project I'm involved in, once I break that mile mark, the good ideas flow. And I can stop and capture them. In never worked when I *intended* to remember that idea for a brilliant article or course…

You never know where or when the good ideas you've been working on are going to bubble up and spring forth. And if you don't capture your ideas when they happen, you may not ever get them again.

Ideas are like those bubbles… Left to themselves, the soon pop, descend, or blow away.

Ideas are like dreams: how many times have you told yourself, "I'll remember that one in the morning," and in the morning all you can do is vaguely remember you had a dream you were going to remember?

Thoughts, they say, are things—but they're immaterial, intangible, fleeting things. You can change that if you'll make a note.

Surf www.ThinkRich.com * Quantum Business Acceleration, $197 value gift *FREE*

NOTES

Item /passage /page	Insight	Action

Visit HoloMagic.com for $297 in free empowerment gifts

You Can't Win Trying Not To Lose

One of the ironies about the Law of Attraction is that it works. Which means *whatever* we hold in mind we attract. Which means if we hold fear, lack, worry, and defeat it will surely manifest in our circumstances, no matter what calamities must happen to make it complete.

No matter how good you *really* have it… You will make sure, with the energy and quality of your thoughts, to experience it. That's Quantum Law, "The observer affects the observed."

The simile situation is the teaching of Job in the Christian Bible. The passage opens up describing the hugely satisfying life of a successful, God-fearing man. As the passage says, "this man was the greatest of all the people of the east" (Job 1:3).

Not believing in your potential, believing you're really a fraud, is a deadly thing.

That which we fear we cause to pass. Those are Job's words: "The thing that I fear comes upon me, and what I dread befalls me" (Job 3:25)."

Do you get the feeling he was suffering all along? One can be, in fact, extremely blessed, but never *feel* the joy it's supposed to bring, bringing into their experience that which they tune their consciousness to.

It's like they say in trading stocks, options, and futures, you've got to play to *win*. You can't play *not to lose*, or that's exactly what you attract. There's an entirely different philosophy, opportunity window, etc that takes you to a different direction.

You play a different way; you get different results. You yourself - though you may not dream it, and would fight vehemently against the idea – create those different outcomes. That's your character made manifest.

It's everywhere you go... From your life and career to your romantic life...

I just heard a song, "The Rose," and it talks about this. Listen to a few words of wisdom here...

> It's the heart afraid of breaking
>
> that never learns to dance,
>
> It's the dream afraid of waking
>
> that never takes a chance,
>
> It's the one who won't be taken
>
> who cannot seem to give...

"It's the heart afraid of breaking that never learns to dance." What we, fear we create. What we want, we push away. It may be totally unconscious, but it's still a very powerful emotion.

That's why we install experiential metaphors that have REAL challenges and risks, like firewalks, eating fire, and breaking boards in our group work. It helps us viscerally challenge and expose fear for the imposter it is...

Once you experience breakthrough success in one impossible dimension – remember, *fire burns* – it suddenly becomes easier to see the make-believe barriers you've been projecting for exactly what they are. You have an experience of conquering incredible odds successfully.

It's all about breakthrough. It's about getting you in an environment where we learn and demonstrate the *mind* is the greatest determinant of failure or success. "Think you can, think you can't, either way you're right," says Henry Ford.

And think you can or think you can't – that's where you put your faith and belief. And that in which you believe at the subconscious level – that which you really believe, not what you shout at pep rallies – serves as your outgoing energy into the holoverse.

Then, like ripples returning back on their source, that is what the Law of Attraction brings back. It's the way the Quantum world works. The corollary of "the observer affects the observed" is that we either get conscious and attract what we want, or worry about what we don't want, which will appear to come all by itself, even if it takes Gods and devils to make it happen...

When we talk of *act as if,* we're not talking about false bravado. We're talking about how whatever you've decided you want to do, you accept yourself as that new person, and you go into action doing it. Not fearing you're secretly not worthy, because that's what the subconscious picks up on and translates into situation, circumstance, and events. No, you're in action *doing* it.

The line goes, "It's the one who won't be taken who never learns to give," and it's the one cowering and unable to pull up self-confidence who never creates, contributes, and receives...

But he or she could.

Surf www.ThinkRich.com * Quantum Business Acceleration, $197 value gift *FREE*

Notes

Item /passage /page	Insight	Action

THE END

Index

Any Time I've Ever Left Something Undone It's Never Got Done
Ask The Question From A Totally Different Viewpoint
Education Continues Forever-Learning Enough In An Hour
Eternity Happens In The Moment
Even Shakespeare Spoke Of The Mind-Environment Connection
Evidence Of Spelling Error Points To Mind-Environment Connection
From Darkness To Light, The More Freedom You Enjoy
He Preferred To Pay Forty Thousand Dollars Rather Than Fly For Free
I Just Saved Myself From Having A Grudge Against That Guy
It Will Always Be This Time
It's Never Living We Should Fear
It's Not All About Money, Crying In The Ecstasy
Prepare Today For The Inevitable Tomorrow
Savor the Sweetness Of A Moment's Rain
The Not-Too-Symbolic Letting Go
There's More Than Brain Entrainment Today
Time In The HoloMagic Quantum Universe
You Can Change That If You'll Make A Note
You Can't Win Trying Not To Lose

Ted Ciuba is also the author of the incredible modernization and empowerment of Napoleon Hill's success classic, *Think & Grow Rich!*

The New Think & Grow Rich

Ted Ciuba

Quantum Business Acceleration Headcoach
Author Sub 4 Minute Extra Mile Series

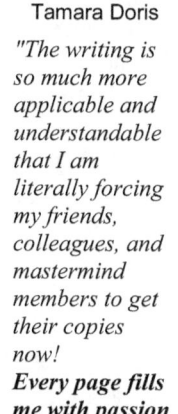

Tamara Doris

T.J. Rohleder

"This is **more than just a revamp with modern examples** - it radically transforms the vision by adding new gender, cross-cultural and international issues to the mix, including new material to include both science and genetics, as in the Quantum reality of accelerating income and wealth. An excellent re-do of a classic financial inspirational guide."

"The writing is so much more applicable and understandable that I am literally forcing my friends, colleagues, and mastermind members to get their copies now! **Every page fills me with passion and revs me up!**"

"I picked up Ted's book -- AND I WAS SHOCKED AND AMAZED! I sat there and began going through it ... and all of a sudden looked up and over 3 hours had gone by!!! I quickly read it from cover to cover within 2 days and then turned around and did it again! Ted has done a truly amazing thing, by totally re-writing this powerful classic. Every entrepreneur and business owner simply MUST have Ted's book!"

"You Are Closer To A Million Dollar$ Than You Now Dream!"

This is the modernized, quantum empowered version of Napoleon Hill's success classic, *Think And Grow Rich!*

#1 Best-Seller

An instruction manual to *consciously* direct the Quantum universe to manifest your positive desires."

Napoleon Hill Overlooks Ted Ciuba

Physical, Kindle. iStore

Are you ready for breakthrough progress overnight?!

- Engage with *The New Think And Grow Rich* - empower yourself! Start exactly where you are - no experience, no education, no cash required! Discover how to…
- Trigger the *law of attraction* AND *self-fulfilling prophecy*!
- Apply insights of secret "combination" for your immediate success
- Direct the Quantum universe to deliver success
- Unleash that powerful "HoloMagic c^2 factor" to accomplish your pursuits in a fraction of the time, with a quanta of the effort

Mark Whyborn, UK

"I have read The New Think And Grow Rich and there is a HUGE improvement (so much more insight) in the new updated version!

"Once you learn the formula to riches, you can apply it to accelerate your income into the stratosphere!"

Order now, for you and your company &your loved ones.

www.ThinkRich.com/book

Additional Sub 4 Minute Extra Mile Volumes Available!

The entire line of training sessions in The *Sub 4 Minute Extra Mile* Series!

Entire Collection!

Sub 4 Minute Extra Mile Series

http://ThinkRich.com/sub4min

Full details on each title!
Complete your collection!
Give a meaningful gift!

Volume: Title
001: Create Your Life By Design
002: Know Your Purpose, Embrace Adventure
003: That HoloMagic c2 Factor
004: A Single Reason Why
005: Same Winds, Different Direction
006: The Day Superman Died
007: Do Something Different
008: Be Encouraged By The Shortness Of Life
009: Celebrate Today!
010: His New Business Called Him On The Phone
011: The Mind-Environment Connection
012: How To Get Back Up Every Single Time You're Knocked Down
013: "Use my time! Use my time! USE my time!!"
014: The Price Of The Holy Grail
015: What Do People Want Bad Enough They're Willing To Pay For It?
016: The Power In Calm Aggressiveness
017: Intention Trumps Time
018: Defy Reality, Re-Define Possibility
019: Sell Your Soul For Security
020: The Blur Between The Impossible And The Possible

021: These Are The Prayers Napoleon Hill Prayed
022: From Writing Poetry To Crashing 747s
023: Develop Your Empowerment Signals To Get Instant Boost And Focus
024: The Law Of Action Triggers The Law Of Attraction
025: It Will Always Be This Time

Yours, *free!*

101 Success Secrets

From *The New Think And Grow Rich!*

Welcome!

>   101 Success Secrets
>   101 Training Sessions
>   101 Seconds Each

101SuccessSecretsFromTheNewThinkAndGrowRich.com

Celebrating the publication of *The New Think And Grow Rich* - **Revised Edition** - author Ted Ciuba put these video secrets together and makes them freely available to you. $197 value, *FREE!*

- 101 Success Secrets
- 101 Training Sessions
- 101 Seconds Each

Turn your life around. Stay focused. Achieve your dreams.

It's **all yours *free*!**

"How Quickly Would Your Life Improve If You Began Using The Untapped 90% Of Your Brain To Bring You Wealth?!"

Revolutionary neuroscience driven!

Quantum Leap Mind Training
Installs *NEW Think and Grow Rich* Philosophy In You Effortlessly!

**Amazing new neurosynergist® technology is a Quantum Leap above ordinary remedies!
In the words of a Stanford neuroscientist, it makes change easy through "structural brain change"!**

Wealth Programming
"Strap on your headphones, change your world!"

Wealth Programming is the *only* neural repatterning system in the world based on the proven principles of *The NEW Think And Grow Rich* using the patented neurosynergist® sound technology.

Dives to the depths of your *delta* subconscious, at the level where you connect with HoloCosm, and reprograms ou to knowledge, skills, & attitudes of achievers,

➢ Unleash the 90% realm of the brain that few people access and find your fortunes using the principles of *The NEW Think and Grow Rich!*...
➢ Put this cutting-edge, powerful, neural repatterning system to work for you!

Visit:
www.QuantumMindTraining.com

Who Else Would Like To Have *The NEW Think and Grow Rich* Author Ted Ciuba Motivate and Train Your Group?

Schedule permitting, Ted Ciuba welcomes keynote, speaking and training invitations from businesses, organizations, associations, and promoters.

The quantum performance message of *The New Think And Grow Rich* and *Sub 4 Minute Extra Mile* is perfectly suited to anyone in pursuit of money, a career, sales, and a life!

Through a brief but thorough pre-event questionnaire, Ted Ciuba makes each presentation unique to each group.

To discuss opportunities and arrangements contact our organization by email at events@holomagic.com or from the website at www.HoloMagic.com

Ted Ciuba On Stage In LA

ADDITIONAL COPIES OF

THE NEW THINK AND GROW RICH

AT A DISCOUNT

This book reveals the key to unlocking your wealth, the secret formula to riches, the combination to the vault of abundance in modern terms and in modern ways.

Individuals have bought this book, looking to forge their destiny of riches. They've in turn, bought this book for their friends and family members, hoping to impart the mystical magic of its power. Suggested it to their employers, to distribute the book and train on it.

Entrepreneurs and coaches buy this book for their team members. Insurance and real estate companies buy this book for all the personnel in their organizations. Multi-level companies and all sales forces make this book required reading - to achieve outstanding success at any age. Motivators and business opportunities experts demand you read this book.

Companies have even bought this book and *given* it to their *customers*! Talk about an enlightened company!

To get a discount on multiple copies visit…

www.HoloMagic.com/ntr/multiple.html

www.ingramcontent.com/pod-product-compliance
Lightning Source LLC
Chambersburg PA
CBHW061516180526
45171CB00001B/197